Because I Said Yes Series Vol. 1

The Truth About College:

The Good, The Bad, & The Ugly

By

Sylvia L. Caver

Table of Contents

Acknowledgements

To God Almighty who I owe everything. To my mother who loved me unconditionally, stood by me through the good and bad, and never gave up on me. You are the wind beneath my wings. To my father. To my two reasons to live, my children. To my brother Shelton who has been my backbone. To my best friend Bridget C. whom I love very much. To my faithful trusted friend and confidant Mrs. Pamala Shanks. To my entire family. To my church family and pastor Darron Chapman.

And I would like to give a special thanks to the people who prayed me through the storm when everyone else rejected me: Pastor Eddie Simpson, Pastor Annissa Nobles, Apostle Loutricia Lee, Pastor Theodis McSwain, Apostle Mafalda Taylor, Bishop Charles & Pastor Verlean Chambers, Yolanda Coleman, Prophetess Vickie Fluker, Apostle Greg & Lyndsey Adams, Apostle Sydney Dortch, Bishop Reggie Miller, and Pastor Bettie Robinson of New Found Faith.

And last but not least, the Waynesboro-Wayne County Library Staff and any young person who has lost their way in life and don't know how to pick up the pieces. May God bless you all and I hope this book touches someone.

Introduction

In the beginning I was just like any other normal child. I had dreams, goals, and aspirations. My mother poured everything she could pour into me for me to excel in life. My mother instilled in me at an early age the importance of education. And when I had graduated from high school, I thought that day had finally came. But in reality, I would soon find out that we can make plans all we want to in life and they will never come to pass. Only God Almighty can direct our paths. What do you do when everything in your world has went wrong? What do you do when everything you touch crumbles? What do you do when your life, your dreams, and all of your hopes have been shattered? You look to the hills from whence all my help cometh. My help cometh from the Lord!

I wrote this book to share my testimony with the world so that someone who has lost their way will be able to find the light at the end of the tunnel. I won't young people to understand that even if they have made mistakes in life, God is able. Because I too was one of those who had lost their way. I was just like the prodigal son. But I found out as you will find out in this book, if He have to reach way down, Jesus will pick you up! This is my true-life story of how Jesus had mercy on me, and reached down to the bottom of the barrel, and saved me. Names have been changed to protect the privacy of others involved.

Chapter 1: It Was Like A Dream

When I graduated from High School in 2002, I had so many scholarships to help pay for me to go to college. I had a $20,000 scholarship to the private college of my choice for Speech and Debate. I had over $4,000 in money I won from the Southern Christian Leadership Congress (Baptist Association). I had a $200 Ebonette Club Scholarship, and I had graduated from high school with honors, many awards, and medals. . The fame of the young girl from Buckatunna, who went to Nationals in St. Louis Missouri, and won 3rd place in the speaking contest had spread everywhere. I was in all of the newspapers, on NBC News, I sit on platforms with Jesse Jackson, and Martin Luther King Jr.'s son. Churches were calling on me to say speeches to the youth everywhere. Sometimes they would have me to sing too. The hype behind my name was surreal. I remember being so excited that I had gotten so much money for school for speaking, especially the debate scholarship. I was so excited because every since the third grade I dreamed of being both a prosecuting lawyer and civil attorney that could sue people. I always knew I wanted to practice criminal law and civil law. This was truly a dream unfurling for me.

The first day, I sat foot on the college campus was during orientation. The orientation leaders separated the prospective students from their parents and took us all on tours. My soon to be coach whom I liked to call Slim Shady, personally escorted me around the school. My mom was very nervous at first. When she was in her group, the other parents turned their nose up at my mom and wouldn't socialize with her throughout the school tour. Meanwhile my coach had taken me by the theatre department and the music department, and all of them offered me scholarships. So I had scholarship offers for Speech and Debate, Theatre, and Music. However, at this school, you were only allowed to have one talent scholarship. The rule said you couldn't stack scholarship. Angry that the other departments were trying to recruit me for themselves, My coach Slim Shady came and got me and told them to stay away from his new debater. And that's when all the faculty, parents, and students met in the courtyard for lunch. There was a student organization representing all of the Black students on campus that asked me to come tell them about myself. They told me that they had a choir. I told them that I love to sing. So they asked me to sing right then in front of everyone. That's when I let out a loud harmonious waling of I know I've Been Changed Pace Sisters style. Much to my surprise, The entire faculty and staff, students, and parents were applauding me and giving me a standing ovation. Those snobby parents were asking who is that girl? Where did she come from? That's when my mother proudly exclaimed, "That is my daughter Sylvia. She has been accepted here on full scholarship with several other scholarship offers and grants!" Man if you could seen the look on their faces then. They flooded around my mom asking her a pile of questions. How did your daughter get all of those scholarships? Where is she from? Yep, things were looking good. After my solo debut, my coach came and personaly ushered me to the table seat beside him with all of the debate team members. Then he arranged for my mom to sit with us. And my coach literally ate the food out of my plate. Yep... Slim Shady was alright with me. My coach told me "Sylvia, from here on, all you have to worry about is keeping your grades up, wearing nice suits, carrying a briefcase, and a pair of shades. And that, sounded like a great plan to me....

Chapter 2: The Dream Unfurled

In August of 2002, college begin at the private Christian College. I had met my roommate and she did hair. We hit it off great. First things first, I had to pick out a major. I met with coach Slim Shady. I told him I wanted a major that would guarantee me a job and help me with law school. Coach Slim Shady encouraged me to major in Speech Communication. I remember specifically asking him, "Can I get a job with a degree in Speech Communication?" Slim assured me that I would. And because I was on the debate team, the school offered an advanced program. A dual major in Speech Communication and Theatre. That was my new major. So my coach scheduled my classes, and sent me to the bookstore to pick up my books. Man, I learned quickly that books for college are expensive. I spent almost $300 on books alone. A sacrifice for my education.

Now what I liked about college already, is that I could pick when I wanted to go to my classes. This was great for me because it gave me the option to sleep late everyday unlike in High school. And also I learned that there were no curfews. I could stay up as late as I wanted. My mom was not there to tell me when to go to bed or what to do. I quickly developed an attitude that I was grown and I didn't need my mother anymore. She would only just hold me back. I remember how I would tell her over the phone, "Mom I'm grown now. I can do whatever I want." I was young, attractive, had good credit, scholarships, a bright future, ambition, and the world was at my fingertips. My mom had to definitely understand, that it is my time now.

Now when I left home, I set a goal for myself---to study hard and keep my grades up. Do whatever it takes to not go back to the oppressive home I came from in Buckatunna. Yep this country bird was about to fly. Before we started our first classes, my coach had a debate team meeting. It was here that I met all of my debate teammates. I felt so nervous. These had to have been the smartest kids I had ever met. We went around the room one by one, telling our majors, where we were from, and what our career goals were. There was so much diversity in that room. I quickly noticed that I was almost the only Black student on the team, with the exception of a beautiful bright skinned girl name nanna. She was highly intelligent as well as everyone else on the team. This was definitely the smartest of the smart people on campus. My coach informed my teammates how I had never actually debated before. Everyone crowded around me with curiosity and told me that I would learn to love it. So when we left out of the debate meeting, I asked my coach could he sign me up for classes that would help me be a better debater. Coach Slim was so excited, He signed me up for an Argumentation and Debate class. Yes I was determined; I would become the greatest debater.

The first class I went to was my English Class. I quickly noticed that Chip from the debate team was in my class. I walked in and smiled and waved at everyone. I noticed right away that several of the guys were checking me out. I pulled off my hat and my cardigan, and flashed my pretty white teeth. English class was a breeze. The first thing we learned about was writing that was redundant and sounded remedial. My teacher complimented me on my writing strength. And by the end of class, I had made four new friends.--A dark skinned intelligent girl name Big P who wanted to be a doctor. Big P was majoring in Biology. Then there was Polyester who stood 6'5 and was cut like a diamond-- he would soon become my boyfriend. Polyester was on scholarship for journalism and had dreams of being a wealthy journalist. And there was Flem. Flem was short and stocky built with strong shoulders and arms. And we were friends, but we would later on get into so many arguments. Yes, I was blossoming. I had met so many people and was quickly making friends.

After classes, my coach scheduled our first debate practice. Now everyone on the debate team was experienced except for me. Even the new students had competed in debate tournaments in highschool before. However, I had not had any experience and I was very nervous. The first type of debate I learned was Parliamentary Debate. And it was so exciting. But in reality, I really sucked at it because I really was like a fish out of water. To make matters worse, my teammate Chip, constantly reminded me of everything I did wrong and how I sucked. He went on to embarass me everytime anyone gave me an ounce of a compliment. He would rudely interrupt them and felt obligated to tell everyone that I was a true novice--you know someone who didn't know what they were doing. Yep, right from the start, Chip was bad. And soon I would learn, that if one bad apple touches another, it makes that apple bad too. One bad apple can ruin the whole bunch.

But coach Slim Shady saw that I had strengths in Individual Events. So he had students to teach me how to do individual events for poetry and prose. I took to them like a natural. Then my coach talked to me about my background in platform speaking. Thats when Slim discovered I was a natural at Persuasive speaking. So my coach instructed me on how to write a persuasive speech and I practiced my acting skills on the other stuff. And for the beginning of my debate career, my events were Parliamentary Debate which I sucked at, Persuasive Speaking, Duo Interpretation, and Poetic Interpretation. The first poems I performed were by Maggie Estep: The Sex Goddess of the Western Hemisphere. Yet still, Chip continued to remind me that I didn't know anything, and made me feel worthless and unwelcome on the debate team. So this was the start of my Debate Team Epic.

Chapter 3 The Dirty Hare

My first class taught by my coach Slim Shady was Public Speaking 101. It was in this class that I first met someone I learned to be a hater named the Dirty Hare. She literally stalked and harassed me throughout my collegiate debate career. She was very opinionated and annoying. The first day of Public Speaking class I arrived late and accidentally forgot to take my hair roller out my front bang. There was an overwhelming fear all over me. I was away from home trying to be somebody and surrounded by people whom I didn't know. I was so scared. I stood out like a sore thumb. The coach made a comment about how he didn't like people being late. And I responded, "Ahh Coach, But I'm Black. We're Always Late!" Without asking her for her two cents, the Dirty Hare butts in, "Speak for yourself!" So I said yeah but you're old and you like don't have anything to do." Dirty Hare replies, "Who are you calling old?" Mind you at this time she was well over 50. So Coach Slim Shady breaks this convo up and says, "Sylvia I want you to do your report for our upcoming assignment on stereotypes and Mrs. Hare, I want you to take care of Sylvia."

And that's how some of the most miserable moments of my life started. From that simple request from Coach Slim Shady, Dirty Hare felt like she had the liberty to tell everyone she was responsible for me. I could tell right then, from that instant, that this old hag had personal interests in me. And it was from this moment forth, that the Dirty "Old" Hare, went around the entire campus telling everyone that she was my personal mentor. Howbeit, the school Student Support Services, never officially assigned her to me as my official mentor. Infact, they assigned someone entirely different. Nevertheless, that did not stop the Dirty Hare from riding my coat tails and telling people she was my mentor. Oh from that moment on, the Dirty Hare would go out her way to get in all of my business, harass me to do her homework, and literally stalk me at times. I found our relationship to be quite abusive instead of a mentoring relationship. I noticed that right away, in classes that the Dirty Hare took with me, she would go out of her way to expound on any comment that I originally had made---even if it was obvious she didn't know what in the hell she was talking about. Yes... The Dirty Hare was a hater... But that will all come out a little later in this story....

Meanwhile, Coach Slim Shady had us to continue having debate practice for the upcoming tournaments. I had discovered that each of my Individual Events were ten minute speeches that I had to memorize with properly cited sources. Much to everyone's amazement, I had a natural raw talent for memorizing speeches quickly. It only took me three days to memorize a speech. Coach Slim and the team was shocked when I came back to rehearsal with my Persuasive speech entirely memorized and a portion of my Poetry event memorized. The team went ecstatic. But of course, Chip still had something negative to say. He informed me that I didn't need to expect to win any awards for my first tournament. And you know what, as often as Chip would put me down, no one for the first part of my debate years would come to my rescue. Chip continued to give out verbal put downs without anyone reprimanding him.

Chapter 4 A Friendly Game

The best part of the week was Friday. On Fridays the schools always served the best food--Fried catfish fillets. And the food in the cafeteria was always all you can eat, which probably explained why the meal plans were so expensive. Other than fried chicken on Wednesday, the food in the school cafeteria really sucked. For Christ's sake they didn't even serve real burgers. We had to eat veggie burgers on the other days which were very gross. Other than that, we had a mediocre salad bar or french fries and mystery meat to always look forward to. So fried fish on Fridays was one of the things I learned to look forward to. Also, sometimes my professors would let us out of class early on Fridays because they wanted to get to the cafeteria to get some of that good old fried fish too. Fried fish and early dismissal from class was great! Now in the cafeteria is where it was on and popping. I sat at the table with all my friends--Big P who was very Afrocentric, TreeTop, Polyester, his brother Brad, Flem, an accounting major Layla, and my roommate Lisa. Let me tell you, we talked the most trash. Me, Big P, and Polyester all liked and wrote poetry. Flem loved to argue. But I was on scholarship for debate, so I became the target for most of the heated discussions. Everyones objective was to beat me in an argument. And let me tell you; they would team up and try to beat me. It was hilarious and fun to see them trying to beat me. This would last for hours. Even after we had finish eating in the cafeteria, we would go sit under the BSU (Baptist Student Union) porch and continue the heated conversation. And when the gang saw that I would not give in, we all decided that we would settle this on the basketball court.

Now after eating and arguing till we couldn't argue anymore, we would all go back to our dorms and put on our tennis shoes and sweats. Then we would all meet back up at the gym. Tree Top was 6'9 and was on basketball scholarship for the college. Polyester was 6'5 and turned down a basketball scholarship to the college. He had terrible acne and bucked teeth with a huge gap. Flem was almost my height--5'5 and also had a basketball scholarship. Layla my roommate was an education major and didn't have time to hang out with us due to her heavy class load. Plus she had a lot of pretty girl tendencies. Big P loved attention from the guys but she was not down with that getting sweaty thing. Lisa had pretty girl tendencies to so she went back to her dorm room. But me, I was a pretty girl who didn't know she was pretty. I was a true tomboy. And I was about to show these boys how country girls get down on the B-Ball court. Now Polyester was the most skilled player by far. His basketball skills were sick. Tree Top picked me for his team. So it was me and Tree Top verses Polyester and Flem. To everyone's surprise, I was very aggressive on the court. I could hold my man and could rebound very well. No one saw that coming. No one except Tree Top. I guess he kinda knew because he was much older than us. Tree Top was 28 yrs old and the rest of us were all 18. But that was their loss and our gain. We won and they loss. And from that point on, me and Tree Top really rubbed it in their faces. And this was so much fun. After the gym closed down at 12 every night, me and my crew sat on dorm porches just talking, laughing, and telling jokes. We all sat there until the sun would rise. I remember the first night I sit outside with everyone, I said I was cold. Infact, I was always cold at that college. Thats why grandma had brought me sweatsuits and gave me her dialysis blanket. When I said I was cold, Flem took his coat off and wrapped it around me. Tree Top said he was going to his dorm room. But Polyester and Flem decided to walk me and Big P to our dorms. I gave Flem his coat back and went to my room. When I got back in my room, the phone was ringing. Who would be calling me at 5:30 in the morning.... I answered.... It was Polyester.. And thats when things started to get a lil interesting.

Chapter 5 Strange Romance

Now I really was a pretty girl who didn't know she was pretty at all. I didn't believe in wearing makeup at all. I wore jogging suits most of the time. When I learned how to take t-shirts and wrap my head up, that became my signature hairstyle. I hardly ever combed my hair. You would never catch me in a pair of high heels like the other girls. I did not wear the big dangly earrings either. I wore carmex lip balm and stud earrings. But things suddenly got weird when I noticed that Polyester would have clothes on that were similar to mine. And instead of sitting in the back of the classroom where he usually sat with Flem and Big P, he moved to the front of the classroom by me. If I had on a gray head rag, I noticed Polyester would have on a gray head rag. Infact, he just started wearing head rags everyday... This really annoyed me. So I decided that I had to start combing my hair and stop wearing the head rags. So I did the only reasonable thing a young lady could do in this situation, I started wearing my hair in two pigtails pulled to the back everyday. Now copy that Mr. Polyester!!!

Next, Polyester started popping up at my dorm lobby on his own to hang out with me. He said he was trying to hook me up with Flem, his best friend. But its funny how we always ended up talking about everything except Flem. We would talk about our poetry, career goals, our classes, people we didn't like, and everything else. We had so much to talk about. Infact we had so much to talk about that we never had time to talk about Flem at all. From there, me and Polyester started going to the weight room to work out together. It happened by chance one day we were working out when Polyester's shirt accidently came up. Oh My God! He had muscles in places I did not know people could have muscles. He had the body of an Olympian. He was literally cut and ripped up like a diamond. Everything was defined--Even his latissimus dorsi. I quickly turned my head like I didn't see all of that. When we went back to the dorm that night, I called a meeting in the dorm room with Big P and all the other girls. I went crazy telling them how fine and ripped up that boy was. It was from this moment on, me and Polyester was unseparable. If my mom would come to see me, she had to see Polyester too. He went with me everywhere. He even would go in the women's department and pick out clothes for me that made me look more feminine. One weekend when my mom came and got me, I invited Polyester to come to my house for the weekend too.

When Polyester came to my hometown he experienced a culture shock. It was nothing like the Delta where he was from. There was lots of land. There were farms everywhere. And my family cooked loads of food. My family cooked so much food, as if they were feeding an army. This was new to him, but not to me. When we got back to school that Sunday, Polyester stopped me. He said he had to tell me something. I told him okay. But I interrupted him and told him how I didn't come to college to get a boyfriend. That I was going to focus on my grades. He asked me to be quiet. He explained how he had found the perfect girl. And that it was me. I told him nooooooooo!!! But He screamed out loud as he could possibly scream, I want you Sylvia. Then He Kissed me. I kissed him back. Okay What just happened here I thought. This is so wrong. He was supposed to have been hooking me up with Flem, but now this. How are we going to explain this to our friends now...

Later on Polyester had his older sister to fix my hair one night because pretty much I tried to always hide my feminity. And thats when the secret was revealed. His sister exclaimed, "So this is the girl my brother has been talking about all the time." I was shocked. All this time Polyester was supposed to be hooking me up with his best friend flem, when he secretly wanted me for himself.

Word got around campus pretty quick that Polyester and I were a couple. One day the Dirty Hare pulled me to the side and asked me why was I even talking to someone like Polyester. She said I could do so much better for myself. She didn't like how he looked. She didn't like the shoes he wore or how he dressed. She was all up in my business. I guess she felt authorized because she had declared herself my official mentor. She said Polyester wasn't good for me. And although its' sad to say, later on I found out that Polyester didn't mean me any good at all.

Meanwhile, the day for my first debate tournament had finally arrived. We left on a Thursday morning for Shreveport Louisiana to compete in the LSU Swing Tournament. We traveled in vans that the school had rented. Coach Slim Shady drove one, and a student drove the other. I was so scared and very nervous. The older debate students pulled rank for seats in the front of the van. I had to sit in the very back almost completely on a tire hump with Chip. I was the only black student on the van. One of the senior students started talking to coach Slim Shady about race relations. He said he didn't understand why black people were demanding slave reparations. And he then went on to clarify that Affirmative Action was discrimination against white people. Coach Slim Shady told him, "Don't you dare say that. What our country has done to black people is like putting them in the fighting ring with their hands tied behind their backs and telling them to fight. It is an unfair fight from the beginning. Affirmative Action levels the playing field."

From that point on, other students begin to chime in on their opinions against Affirmative Action. The debate was very heated. I just sit there in my seat quietly and stared out of the window. I took in the view of all the places I had never seen before. I was scared yet fascinated. Debate was taking me further away from home than I had ever been. One thing for sure, I certainly was not in little ole Buckatunna anymore.

And your gift will make room for you and bring you before great men.....

Chapter 6 Tournaments

As the school year progressed, I continued to practice my debate skills. People around me, in my classes, and even my professors begin to notice how articulate I had become. I noticed that my vocabulary became very advanced. I was trying very hard to not sound like a pedantic to my peers. I had no problems conveying my messages in conversations, classroom discussions, or in social settings. My mind was like a sponge. I was soaking in so much knowledge. While my peers were going to the night clubs, I would be in my dorm room with a book up to my nose. I devoted most of my time to studying. All the hardwork paid off when I got my report card. A and B honor roll and sometimes straight A's. And inspite of what Chip had said about me, the hardwork was starting to pay off on the debate tournaments.

It was our third tournament for the year. By now I had gotten use to leaving campus early in the morning and driving for 12 hours or more to our motel. Then we would go to bed late and get up early again the next morning to go to a college I had never been to before. While wearing high heels, me and the other competitors would have to walk all over the college campus to perform events. We would compete all day and return to the motel late. This routine lasted over a span of four to five days. We always came back home on Sundays. It was exciting to me. I loved every moment. Meeting hundreds of new people, seeing sights I never saw before, flying on the jets and airplanes, and riding the vans. It was a breathtaking experience. And by this time, I finally begin to get recognition for all of my hard work. I finally started to win some awards. The first time I won an award at the tournament it was for persuasive speaking. Later I would learn this was my strongest event. Later on I would take the headline on the front of the local newspaper.

During my time of traveling on speech and debate tournaments, I went through a process of changes. At first I didn't win any awards. But in the middle of the season, I begin to rack up lots of awards. I won high ranking awards for persuasive speaking, and novice awards for poetry, prose, and public debate. And just like that, my name began to be in the local newspaper every month for the many awards I had won. People I didn't even know began to take notice of me. People on the faculty and staff of the school begin to show me their support. When I think about it all I feel like a bomb had went off and I had blown up and became famous all over again. It was so amazing. My grandmother was so proud of me. She would buy me an entire wardrobe of expensive clothes to wear on the tournaments. I was the only grandchild she did that for. My mom was so proud of me. She couldn't stop talking about my accomplishments for a single day. God had made me so successful. And although I had made my claim on the collegiate circuit as a fierce competitor, things were about to become very difficult. This was the beginning of my adversity I had to endure to get my education. I faced rejection from my peers, abuse from my jealous boyfriend, and became the target of a lot of undeserved animosity.

Yea though I walk through the valley of the shadows of death, I will fear no evil, For thou art with me.

Chapter 7 Ignorant and unlearned

Looking back over my life I wonder how did I make it. How did I survive all of those traumatic events and still obtain my education. I have matured enough now to realize the living God kept me through it all. On my journey, I learned so many life lessons. And after that first year of being on the debate team, I learned that it is very lonely at the top. I couldn't settle for staying on the ground with the chickens. I had to mount up wings like an eagle and soar.

I remember having to leave people behind that first year of debate. It first happened when I was sleeping in my dorm room that I shared with Big P. I fell asleep while the tv was playing. When I woke up to go to the restroom, I noticed Big P had left the room. I also noticed that my blue blanket that my grandmother who was on dialysis had gave me--- I noticed it was missing. I decided to walk downstairs to the lobby to see if I could find Big P. When I made it to base of the steps on the first floor, I was appalled by what I saw. There was Big P, wrapped up in my grandmother's blue dialysis blanket. She was sitting at the table talking to my boyfriend --Polyester. She had just said she was going to give him a massage while reading him a provocative poem. But that plan got canceled immediately when I walked up to them. I begin to curse her for everything I could think of. I snatched my grandmother's blanket off of her. Her and Polyester began to explain they were just hanging out because I was sleep. I so was not buying that line at all. Either way you look at it, I was disrespected on so many levels. And although their plans were throttled for that moment, I found out that later on Polyester and Big P would carry out their plans. But as for me, I immediately requested a private room. And I never trusted Big P again. The first time I ever went to a nightclub was when Big P took me. We had made a pact that we would always protect each other. But after this incident, that agreement became null and void. At this point, It just is what it is because now I was in my feelings. And to make matters worse... When I found her she was reading a provocative suggestive poem she had wrote to my man!!!!

One day I decided that I'd had enough of Polyester. He was doing the usual when I would not let him persuade me to do what he wanted me to do. I would exclaim to him, "Dude I don't need you!' And he would demand that I sit there day and night and give him my full attention so that he could convince me to do things against my will. On this particular day I decided to jerk myself out of his arms and run to my dorm room. When I threw my arms up and mashed my feet in the sofa so I could leave, Polyester slapped me. That was the first time that I had suffered physical abuse from a man. I sit there in tears, shocked and appalled that he had slapped me. He started to explain that it was just an accident. I ran to my dorm room with tears in my eyes. I refused to talk to him or take his phone calls. It was over between us. Thats when he and Big P begin to hang out every day and become very acquainted with each other.

Over the next weeks, I would find Polyester standing outside my dorm room window, demanding that I talk to him. When visitors came to my room, he would startle them with his lurking at my dorm room window harassing me. This kind of harassment went on for several years while I was pursuing my Bachelor's degree. Sometimes I would have to call on my family members to make him stop harassing me. But I was young, ignorant, and unlearned about the ways of the world. If knew then what I know now. Things would have been different.

I remember how things weren't like this with me and Polyester. I remember when we were all playing basketball in the gym. And his best friend took a dirty shot at me and elbowed me in the mouth. He hit me so hard, my tongue blead and purple lumps formed on it with blood clots. But even then I refused to let Flem see me cry. I grabbed my belongings and pulled Polyester off the court. And I told him that Flem was his friend and he'd better handle it. I did not know that the basketball game ended after I left, and that two best friends nearly fought that night over me. Polyester was so different at first. What happened? Or should I say Who came between us?

Chapter 8 The Sophomore Year

I finished the first year of school I decided to enroll in summer school so I could get further alone in the sophomore phase. As I went to summer school before the fall trimester had begun, I met all kinds of new people. I was enrolled in World Literature and Psychology classes. It was in my psychology class that I met Ms. Hazel. Ms. Hazel was an older woman who had retired from working in the corporate business field. She was starting her life all over again by pursuing a second degree in Psychology. She had just gone through a divorce. Now I count it very strange that all of my life, whenever I was in the spotlight or doing well for myself, older women would come along and attach themselves to me somehow. I was already dealing with the dirty hare. Now here comes Ms. Hazel. It started with her asking me to help her with her school work. From then on I would write and type all of her homework. In return, Ms. Hazel would give me generous amounts of money and take me out to expensive restaurants. She would let me order whatever I wanted. All of my expenses were paid by her. From there, Ms. Hazel would take me to professional beauticians and have my hair done and my eyebrows arched. This too was paid for by Ms. Hazel. I didn't understand why Ms. Hazel was giving me shopping sprees and spending so much money on me. I thought she was genuinely helping me because she was my friend. But I would soon find out the truth later on in the Sophomore year.

When I started my sophomore year, I was filled with much enthusiasm. But my heart was still torn. Coach Slim Shady had left me at this college. He took another Coaching job at another school a 1,000 miles away. Later on I would find out the biggest mistake I could have ever made was to not leave that college and go with him to the new school. After all, I had been handpicked and recruited by Coach Slim Shady to come to this Christian College in the first place. I remember when he broke the news to all of us that he was leaving, I cried until blisters came on my face. I was here at this school all alone, with no one to look out for me. No one except for an Old hater who lied and told everyone she was my mentor. Crazy old dirty Hare. I felt despair for a moment. But I learned everything that Coach Slim Shady could teach me in the short time that I was his student.

When our new coach, Mrs. Violet called the first practice meeting for me and my teammates I was already prepared. I had an entire draft for a persuasive speech. Coach Violet begin to tell all of the other students they needed to follow my example. This time, Coach Violet wanted me to try a new event, Impromptu Speaking. I found out that I was a natural at this type of speaking. The year was looking very bright and promising for me. Atleast that's what I thought.

When we got ready to get out of school for a two week break for the holidays, Ms. Hazel strongly impressed upon me that I could stay with her at her house for the entire 2 weeks. So I packed my clothes and left to go stay with her. I had spent several nights with her before. So it shouldn't have been a problem---that's what I thought. But this time, when I stayed, Ms. Hazel began calling me into her bedroom. I entered the room. And that's when Ms. Hazel started taking all of her clothes off in front of me. I told her that I would come back to her room after she was dressed. But Ms. Hazel insisted that I stay. Then she asked me to give her a massage (literally as she stood in front me naked). Suddenly I felt so uncomfortable. I wanted to go home. I ended up scratching her head and massaging her back that night. I lied and told her that I was sleepy so I could escape to my room. On a side note, Ms. Hazel always made me talk on the phone in front of her. I didn't have a cell phone of my own so I had to use her phones. I remember telling my mom to come get me. Ms. Hazel took the phone from me and told my mom not to come get me. She said that I was alright and she would bring me home later. I felt tears roll up in my eyes. I had to endure 3 more nights of Ms. Hazel walking in front of me naked and asking me to massage her before I could escape. One night I had rubbed her feet until she had fallen asleep. I crept into the kitchen and called my mom. My mom could hear in my voice that something wasn't right. She asked me what was wrong and why was I calling so late. I told my mom to please come get me. I was so scared. What if Ms. Hazel caught me calling for help. The next morning I woke up, Ms. Hazel had made me breakfast with pancakes that had fresh blueberries in them. She had fixed me a tall glass of peach moon shine to wash it all down. I had never drunk any alcohol before. I was only 19yrs. old. She kept pressing me to drink it. It tasted sweet and it went down very smooth. Before I could finish the drink my mom was at the door. Ms. Hazel asked me to stay. She tried to impress upon me that I should stay with promises of having so much fun. I told her bye and quickly jumped in my mom's vehicle. I told my mom to drive me straight home. When we had put many miles between me and Ms. Hazel, I told my mom everything Ms. Hazel had tried to do to me with tears in my eyes. I was even more afraid for the safety of my womanhood. But I knew that even then God had sent my mother to rescue me. That wasn't the first time and it wouldn't be the last. And as I begin to breathe again, I thought to myself that I had escaped trouble and things were going to get better from now on. I did not know, that this was the beginning of my troubles in college. Thank God, troubles don't last always.

Chapter 9 Friendly Foes

I had escaped the undercover lesbian Ms. Hazel. Funny thing about it, the Dirty Hare had been warning me that Ms. Hazel was a Lesbian. But I didn't listen because she had a very strange way of making me feel smothered. I just didn't understand why she wanted to be in my business so much. She made it her prerogative to know any and everything she could find out about me. She had to know what my father's name was and his nickname. She wanted to know where I lived. She wanted to know everyone in my family by name. It didn't end there, she needed to know who I was dating, what was my GPA, what was my major, and what classes was I taking. The last one; the one about what classes I was taking was the one that stood out. The old dirty hare would intentionally schedule the same classes I was taking. And when she learned that I had been helping Ms. Hazel with her homework, that's when her motive became a lot more clearer. Without asking me straight up would I do her homework for her, the old dirty hare would pick me up from school. Then she would take me off campus to nice restaurants. Like Ms. Hazel, she would let me order whatever I wanted at her expense. But instead of going, back home to my dorm, the dirty hare would take me to her house. That's where she would manipulate me into doing her school work. I remember how she would do things to intimidate me. Tell me all kinds of stories about people she knew who worked for the FBI. How she had friends in the pentagon. Then she would tell me stories about how she had been in gangs and watched them kill people before. She would go so far to pull her gun out in front of me. She would pull her gold teeth out her mouth and tell me stories about how she got them by selling dope with big time drug dealers. I didn't understand Why. Why did this woman have to target me like this? Just why? This went on for over a span of 3 years. Now I can honestly say, that I thought college was easy. I thought that it was all about knowing how to use book sense. I thought that all I had to do was just go to school, do my school work, and get my degree. But I was beginning to have a very rude awakening. The fact is college has never been easy. Parents send their children to school with big hopes and great aspirations of them becoming an asset to society. But in reality, when you go to school, it is the school of the streets, the school of life, and the school of the hard knocks that teach your children. Their lessons are cruel. College is like sending a sheep into a den of wolves. The fact of the matter is you send your children off to these campuses where they are introduced to drugs and drug dealers, their friends try to pressure them into using alcohol and engaging in risky and promiscuous sexual behaviors, clubs are easily accessible, gang members and non-students can walk on campus at will, some of the teachers try to sleep with their students, and there are people like the Old Dirty Hare who are just looking for someone with a bright mind to take advantage of in every way possible. All of this extra stuff with the pressures of balancing school work and not getting kicked out of school. College is not easy at all!!!

Chapter 10 Trouble In My Way

The Old Dirty Hare was a mean old widow. She was overbearing and constantly sought ways to manipulate me and control my life. I didn't understand why she harassed me so much. Its like she just picked up where Ms. Hazel left off except she was worse. She started out taking me to restaurants in exchange for doing her homework. Then she started manipulating me to mow her yard and act as her personal chauffer. But the picture began to become very clear. The Dirty Hare wanted me to do her HW practically for free. I would get benefits for helping her but they were very cheap benefits. Like she would take me to a bootleg beautician to do my hair. Then the meals started becoming cheap meals accompanied with old hand me down shoes and clothes. It was like she was screaming at me, do my school work for free. I was so tired. I was making the presidents list at school. I was balancing my school work, her school work, work study job, debate team obligations, and I was holding down a full time job at a call center. And just when I thought my load was to heavy, the dirty hare broke her arm. So guess who was responsible for driving from their job early in the morning to pick her up and bring her to school. And guess what, this service was provided as well with no pay. And to make matters worse, there was constant drama on the debate team that always lead back to my teammates motion of me being unworthy of my scholarship---Especially since they did not have a scholarship at all. And I wondered how I could be unworthy of the scholarship when I was winning so many awards consistently. Sometimes my teammates wouldn't even place at the tournaments. I would be the only one who consistently picked up awards.

Sometime, during the unjust stress I was going through because of the Dirty Hare's harassment, things hit rock bottom on the debate team. My Caucasian fellow teammates began to follow Chip's example and lash out at me. They would constantly look for opportunities to say verbal put downs and insults to me. My coach wouldn't give me one on one attention to train me for new events like she did for the other teammates. Because of all of the negativity that was around me on the team, I begin to feel grieved in my spirit. It was getting so hard for me to continue to be a debater. I can remember when one of my teammates was explaining to me that my hair looked bad and how I was inadequate in my events. Her name was Messy Madeline. So I asked her my simple question "Is it because I'm black?" Suddenly there was an awkward silence. Then Madeline replied, "Yes it is because you're black and I wish you and your whole black family and your grandma would go back to Africa!" When she said it, everyone on the team begin to laugh, including coach Violet. I felt so offended. I felt like there was some deep rooted animosity against me. And I felt everyone laughed because they felt the same way about me. And I still feel like our coach should have corrected this behavior. But Coach Violet never did anything to protect me from my team mates. They were allowed to lash out at me at will with their razors for teeth.

From that day on, whenever my team mates said anything that made me uncomfortable, I would still ask them, is it because I'm black. And in response to my question, Madeline's responses were getting even more insulting. Most of the time, the insult would occur because of my rhetorical question to their allegations that I was unworthy of a scholarship. I remember it like it was yesterday. We were in Louisiana at a tournament. We were driving there when we made a pit stop to get food and fuel. When I had got back on the van, my teammates were having a heated argument about the scholarship again. So I comically asked my usual question "Is it because I'm black?" Suddenly I felt fist hitting my body. Richie Rich was hitting me and holding me down up against the window of the van. He hit me in the face while screaming at me, I'm so sick and tired of your antics." My fellow team mate Ricky Bobby, pulled him off of me. And for the rest of the drive to our motel room, I sit on the tire hump gazing out the window with salty tears in my eyes. When we made it to the motel, I told the debate team captain what had happened to me. She told Coach Violet. Coach Violet told Richie Rich to apologize to me for what he had done. Richie never did come and apologize to me at that tournament. As a result of the frustration that was going on around me, I begin to have unwarranted anxiety attacks. I still manage to win first place and other high ranking places in my events, but I was so stressed. When we got back to the campus, I gathered my belongings, my trash, and my awards off of the van and went to my campus apartment. The next day Coach Violet had a letter sent to my campus mailbox. The letter said because I left and went to my room and didn't stay and clean up with the other teammates; I was being placed on punishment for the rest of the year. It said that from that point on I would be responsible for cleaning up the trash on all the vans by myself or my scholarship would be revoked.

I called the Dirty Hare and showed her the letter. The Dirty Hare was so outraged about it. I was the only black student on the team and I was being made to be the team janitor. The Dirty Hare told me to stand up for myself. So I did the best thing I could think of. I went to the library and typed up every incident of bigotry, violence, and mistreatment that I had incurred under the leadership of Coach Violet. I went to the Student Affairs office and submitted my report along with the copy of the letter Coach Violet had written me. To my surprise, Coach Violet was immediately fired. And the vice president asked me if the school expelled Richie Rich would I be satisfied. But I was so young and naive. I felt sorry for a young man who certainly did not like me or have any respect for me. I told the student affairs representative to let him go. I only required that he gave me a written apology for his actions. The school honored my requests, and they had me to sign off on a written contract that clarified they had resolved the issue and I would not pursue taking them to court. Big mistake-- A mistake that would haunt me later on.

After I went to my regular classes, news of how Coach Violet had treated me had made it around the entire campus. Teachers I didn't even know were just walking up to me and apologizing to me on behalf of the school for how I was---Discriminated against. It was this time in my sophomore year, that I suddenly felt like this school wasn't my home anymore. I felt so let down. But when you're at the bottom, there's only one way to go--To The Top!!!! Right???? Atleast that's what I thought. But the

debate season wasn't over with yet, and I still had to get through the rest of the academic year.

Chp 11 The Apartment

After the drama on the debate team was starting to calm down, I just knew my teammates would treat me fairly now and accept me. Wrong Again. Things went from bad to worse not only with my teammates but my roommates too. It really left a bitter taste in my mouth. I remember that I was 19yrs old living in an on campus apartment with my two roommates. One was 28 years old and the other was 24. They were very large women. They professed Christ to me and the public. But they made me feel like they surely didn't know Him. It started when my mom started buying me groceries and snacks just for me. I would come in the apartment, and I would find my roommates eating all of the food my family had just bought for me. And when I question them about it they would laugh in my face. So I would hide my snacks under my bed and put labels on my food. But it didn't make things any better. Yolanda and Tonya would still steal my food. I went to the Dean of Student Affairs and reported what they were doing. They said that I needed to talk to them and try to work it out. The first time I talk to Yolanda and Tonya, they both explained to me that I have to share my food with them because they let me live in the apartment with them. Although I didn't comprehend how that claim had any Merit to it since I was paying the school room and board money to live on campus. So I pressed the matter to them. That's when Tonya explained that I was over reacting. She said she knew I could afford to share groceries with them because she knew I had a scholarship. She explained she did work study in the business office and she saw how much my financial award was. And that I should be grateful because she doesn't get a scholarship. I went back to the Student Affairs office for help. But they didn't really help me. They said they would have a talk with Tonya and Yolanda. I saw that I wasn't getting anywhere, so I stop buying groceries and started variating between eating at the school cafeteria or at Wendy's and Captain D's. My room mates decided that they would ask me for money for them to buy groceries. That was the next con game. But it really hit the fan when I was trying to sleep so that I could focus on my studies. On one particular night I was trying to rest. It was late. Like after 2 in the morning. Tonya and

Yolanda decided to have church services. They turn the music up loud and begin having church. I ask them to calm it down because I was trying to sleep. Tonya (who was the 24 year old ring leader) started approaching me shouting that I was demon possessed. They slung me on the bed. With all of their fat heavy body weight on me, they both sit on me. And they continued a ritual of screaming in my ear for the demon to come out. From that point on, they told me they had to watch me and listen to me every time I prayed. I had no privacy. And that's when I had an epiphany---God loves me too.

This time my room mates were blasting the music at 3:00 in the morning. I walked into the den and I asked them to turn the music down politely. They began to tell me that I had a demon in me and that I had a bad attitude. I told them if they didn't stop I was going to call collegiate administration. Tonya then tells me what goes on in her house stays in her house. So I would like to remind you all that I wasn't filled with the Holy Ghost at this point in my life. And if somebody was doing me wrong, I didn't mind helping them get right. All kinds of curse words came out of my mouth. And when I went to walk out the apartment, Tonya came behind me and grabbed me. She began to hit me. So I fought back. And for a moment it looked like I was winning until Yolanda decided to push me against the wall and restrain me. While I was being restrained, Tonya had picked up my 2 lbs. dumbbell. She was headed towards me to hit me. I was screaming let me go Yolanda. But she wouldn't let me go. But thank God the resident director heard me screaming. And she walked in the room in time to see what they were doing to me, They called security. I told them that I would go stay with my brother until new living arrangements could be made. Now I would like for you to keep in mind, all the furniture in the Apartment was mine. Keep this in mind as I continue with my story.

I received a letter that I was no longer allowed to stay in the Apartment due to using profanity. And Yolanda and Tonya were still living in the Apartment unpunished. Okay, It was time to bring the momma wolf in. My mom came to the college, and requested a meeting with the Dean of Student

Affairs. The dean began telling my mom how my language was so bad, that I had to be punished. Suddenly in the middle of the speech, My mom took her black cane out and wrapped the Dean's desk with all of the power and might that was in her. She said I want to know what is being done about these grown women who put their hands on my daughter who is still a minor. What are ya'll doing to protect my child. And if you can't protect her, then I will involve law enforcement to protect her, because in the eyes of the law these grown women could go to jail. The Dean decided to immediately ban Tanya and Yolanda from staying in the apartment. And as punishment, they were reassigned to the most expensive dorm on the campus. When I went to retrieve my belongings from the apartment, Tonya and Yolanda were sitting on my furniture, using my phone, watching movies with my tv and VCR. And they were using all of my cooking utensils and pots and pans. Yolanda tried to get an attitude with me. But I had security to escort me to collect my property. When I was finished, all that was left was their clothes. And although I felt like I was being treated unfair, I still was okay. I had been placed in a private room that was cheaper than any other dorm at the school.

As I moved into my new room, the Dirty Hare called me. She didn't ask me what happened. She just began to explain to me that I was wrong to fight back. That I made black people look bad to the school. Really! Who told you I was in a fight in the first place? Who told her to go to the faculty as if she was my representative? Why God does this woman feel so entitled to be in my affairs? God knows she was beginning to overwhelm me with her constant pursuit to harass me. And this is where the Dirty Old Hare schemes became even more diabolical. Somehow she got the notion that she could make money.... Big Money off of me and what was going on with me at this school. She began to tell me to document everything that was happening to me--Especially with the debate team. She begin to keep even closer tabs on my affairs. She began to keep records of every phone call of distress and what it was pertaining to no matter how minute. But this too shall pass....

Chapter 12 Have A Drink

My teammates heard about the fight. And for a brief moment, they showed me a little empathy. One of them came forth and told the administration how they heard violent and angry noises coming from our room. But this fake empathy only lasted for a little while. It was time for another tournament. This time we went to a college in Texas. As usual, I rode on the tire hump way in the back of the van. I tried to not say anything to my team mates. I carried my own CD PLAYER with headphones. I just played my music and gazed out the window. We had two new coaches now. One was a lawyer and the other was a journalist teacher who was working on her Doctorate degree. As usual, I racked up quite a few trophies at the tournament. My teammates didn't get as many awards this time. Our coach was pi$$ed off about it. He calm down and took us all out to eat at Outback Steakhouse. When we were getting out of the van I asked Ricky Bobby to hold the seat up for me to get out. That's when he replied, "Sure Sylvia and while you at it won't you suck my DICK too." I said what did you say to me? And he clarified again, "Suck my Dick." So I verbally retaliated back at him with all kinds of insults. But my teammates told me to watch my mouth. I grabbed my purse and I walked off behind the building. I sit there and cried. I wanted to go home. And I begin to get weary of being on the debate team with a group of people who constantly made me feel unwelcome.

My lawyer coach came and found me sitting on the ground crying. He was so furious when he had found me. He chewed me out and told me don't ever wonder off from the team like that again. He said he was so scared that they had lost me. He act like he actually cared about me and my safety. I told him what Ricky Bobby had said to me. He told me he would take care of it when we got back to the school. Coach had convinced me to come in the restaurant and eat with all of my teammates. The food was good, but I was crying inside. It was as if something had caused a tiny whole to come into my heart. And my heart was beginning to slowly bleed. What could I do? My heart was bleeding. If I quit the debate team now I would forfeit my scholarship. I still had two more years of schooling to finish.

We made it back home from Texas. But I did not come back home the way I left. I came back with a heart full of sorrows. When we had our next debate practice, our coach had informed every member of the team that they had to verbally apologize to me for how they all had been treating me. All of them apologized willingly accept for one--the one who had been a bad apple from the beginning. Chip. I noticed that his hygiene had gotten so bad. He had on the same outfit for three days or more. His teeth were starting to deteriate. He hadn't shaved in forever. And he had a very strange odor. So I said something to the team captain about it. She called all of the team members in. That's when I discovered that Chip was on drugs. I had no idea, that the location of the school was right in the center of the biggest drug dealing location in the entire State of MS. There was no gate around the campus. And drug dealers from the community literally would just walk on our campus and push their products on young college students. Sometimes a student need a fix of something that would keep them woke all night so that they could study and cram for exams. Oh My God!!! I definitely was not in Buckatunna anymore.

Our team captain decided to do an intervention for Chip. We all took him to the mall and brought him several items of clothing from Abercrombie and Fitch, and the GAP. We had his hair cut and facial hair shaved. Somewhere Chip went and got a bath. And when we got through, Chip looked fantastic. Chip had new look, off the habit, but the same animosity toward me.

That night after we had took care of Chip, me and all of my teammates decided to hang out at the law firm. A conversation was started about alcohol. I innocently told my teammates that I had never drunk any alcohol before or gotten drunk or gotten high. They became very enthused about this. So they convinced me to try some alcohol. I remember they went to the store and left me at the law firm with the guys. They came back with Smirnoff and Coronas. I was scared at first. But my teammates convinced me to have a drink. I had drunk a bottle of Triple Black. It tasted like nasty sprite. They were all laughing and having fun. But my entire mood had changed. I begin to feel sad inside. My head begin to hurt. I ask them to take me back to school. By the time I made it to my room, I could hear thoughts in my head, echoing that I should just die. It was like an uncontrollable sadness came over me. On an impulse, I went to the emergency exit stairs of my dorm. I climbed up as high as the stairs would go. Something said just jump. Jump and it will all be over with. Tears begin to well up in my eyes. I did not want to jump. I went back to my dorm room. I turned on sad depressing music. I played Evanescence My Immortal over and over again. I couldn't sleep. What was wrong with me?

Chapter 13 Coach Dart

I was going into my junior year of schooling. I had the debate team routine down pretty good. We had gotten a new coach. He seemed nice at first. Until I got to know him. His name was Coach Dart. I noticed right away that he was spending personal time with all of the other teammates except me. He was training them in new events. But he never trained me or practiced me in anything. And although Chip wasn't there anymore, and several of the teammates who didn't like me had graduated, there were new recruits who were immediately taught to dislike me. I found out that all it takes is for one person to hate you. And that's enough for them to make everyone else around you follow the leader and hate you too for no good reason at all. Messy Madeline was the new ring leader. It started when we had went on a tournament in Middle Tennessee State University. My teammates sit on my pillows and stepped on them without regard. It really didn't bother me that bad but since I was the newly elected team vice president, I figured I should throw my weight around a lil bit. So I threw a cursing hissy fit. They got the hint to not step on my stuff anymore. When we went to the restaurant, the Old Dirty Hare had called me. Oh yes, at this point she was filling my little head with all kinds of madness and working overtime to keep tabs on me. I told her that I had to lay my phone down because our coach was about to bless the food. When he got through blessing the food I picked the phone back up and resume talking to her. That's when Coach Dart yelled at me and lashed out me. He was screaming that I was so disrespectful and that I had disrespected him, my teammates, and His God. The Dirty Hare heard it all. I laid the phone down while everyone in the restaurant attention was on him yelling at me. He directed me to go outside to stand out in the rain and to continue yelling at me. He made me stand out in the rain while I tried to defend myself and explain to him that I had not talked on the phone while he was blessing the food. Coach Dart did not hear any of my explanations. By this time, my English professor called me and told me she had heard everything he had did and she was having the president of the college call me in a few minutes. I stayed outside and talked to the President of the College---Dr. Mike Byrd. Dr. Byrd told me to tell Coach Dart to meet him in his office first thing Monday morning. So when I went back into the restaurant and informed Coach Dart of what Dr. Byrd had requested. His entire demeanor changed. He said, "You called my boss!" I told him that the Old Dirty Hare and my professor called him when they heard you hollering at me in the rain!"

When we left the restaurant, random white people I didn't even know were walking up to me telling me that my coach is a jerk and they are so sorry that I was having to go through this. I went back to my motel room. Coach Dart summoned me to a personal meeting to try to get me to sign a paper saying I had caused dissension on the team. He said that my teammates had so many complaints about me. That's when it was revealed, the same people who didn't like me on the team had misinformed Coach Dart a bunch of lies about me. I refused to sign the document. When we got back to school, the other faculty in the communications and theater department met with me and Coach Dart to inform how my fellow teammates have been violent with me and constantly illustrated their intolerance of me. He apologized and said he had no idea. That's what happens when one person hates you though. They try to make everyone else hate you too. Coach Dart concluded the meeting that I could not talk on the phone during tournament events. So everything was settled. And for a while, it looked like there would be peace on the debate team for this year of competition.

Meanwhile, down the hall from me in the dorm, my fellow peers were hanging out in our all girls' dormitory. So I went to join them. That's when it became apparent they only had invited me to mock me and pick at me. And the ring leader, an obese stud lesbian named TyTy began to make suggestions to me that made me feel uncomfortable. She explained to me how she felt like I didn't need a man in my life. She said that it sounded like I need the touch of a woman. I felt insulted and disgusted. And I quickly rebutted to her that I am not interested in women and never have been. I like d!@& and d!@& only. And they laughed at me. So I left this little social gathering and went back to my room. You would have thought that everything would have ended there. Nope, Ms. TyTy decides to come to my dorm room and beat on my door and beg me to let her in. I went to the door and screaming at her, I said I do not want to be bothered and I am not interested in girls. Only to hear her say she felt like I needed someone to talk too and that she could help me with my feelings. I locked my dorm room door. Then TyTy decided to place letters under my door. So I called the dorm director. She said she would handle it in the morning. I called my brother. He came and picked me up and I spent every night for a week at his house. And I know that because I was enrolled at a Christian College, men were not allowed in the dorm rooms with women. But this rule did not protect us from lesbians who lived in the dorm with the other women. And although this was my first encounter on campus with harassment from a lesbian, I would soon learn the campus was full of girls who liked girls. I was experiencing a culture shock in the worse way. Lesbianism went against my traditional religious values I was raised by. Now this book is not to debate the LGBTQ movement. I am not a homophobe. But I don't believe in this behavior. And felt it quite insulting and offensive, when my peers tried to force this kind of practice off on me.

Back on the debate team we were getting ready to leave for our last tournament of the year. We would fly to Memphis Tennessee, then to Los Angeles California. We would compete at a tournament there, and then fly to Minneapolis Minnesota. Then we would fly to St. Louis Missouri and compete in a tournament at Webster University. Finally we would fly back home to the Laurel Hattiesburg Regional Airport and drive back to school. When we got on the plane to California, I noticed that Messy Madeline and Phil were having a deep conversation about race relations. They were discussing white people who try to imitate African Americans' culture. And I asked Phil what do you call these sorts of people. That's when Phil replied a White person who tries to be black is just a Whigger. I asked him to explain to me what is a "Whigger". And he clarified that this is a white person who wants to be black. I turned around in my seat and did not say anything to them for the rest of the flight. When I got to the tournament at California Baptist, I noticed that all of my teammates had isolated me and sit to a table with their breakfast and no seat for me. I ate my fruit alone. My teammates had left and went and sit outside with the rest of the assembly without me. That's when the people from the California Baptist College came and escorted me to their section and asked me were there any issues on my team? They said I could sit with them. And that's when I begin to feel an icy coldness and rejection from all of my teammates. My coach was embarrassed. So he came and escorted me back to a seating area with the rest of the team. I didn't win any awards at tis tournament. Later on we all went to the beach. I explained to my coach that I needed to call home to have my family put money in my bank account so that I would have spending money. He said I could use the phone. All of my teammates were using their phones. So it shouldn't have been a big deal. When we were packing up and getting read to leave the motel, I was the first one at the van loading the luggage. Coach Dart commended me for my good behavior. That's when Messy Madeline began to throw my luggage down. I asked her what her problem was. She began to curse at me and try to make me fight her. I was so angry. I refused to fight her. She yelled all kinds of insults at me because I would not let her trick me into fighting her. Coach Dart never reprimanded her. And Messy Madeline was popular with all of the other people on the team. So no one wanted to sit by me or talk to me. And that's how it was for the rest of the tournament.

The Old Dirty Hare said she was looking out for me. She called the Dean of Academic Affairs, and she had her to call Dr. Byrd and tell him everything that was going on. Dr. Byrd personally called me and told me to write down everything that was going on--Even if I had to record it.

We had checked in at our motel in St. Louis at the Sheraton Inn. The motel clerk was named Sylvia like me. We went to bed to get ready for the tournament the next day. I remember feeling so sleepy at the tournament. I would sleep wherever I could in between breaks from events. That's when this lawyer who had come with us pointed out that Coach Dart had brought everyone lunch except me. I had gone the whole day with no food. No big deal though. Coach Dart took the rest of us to dinner at the end of that day. None of my teammate's road in the Jeep with me. I had to ride with the coach and the lawyer everywhere --even back home. I asked Coach Dart could I talk on my phone before we went to bed. He said it was okay. When I tried to go back in my motel room, Messy Madeline and my other teammate had put the deadbolt lock on the door so that my key couldn't let me in. I beat and knocked on the door for over twenty minutes. I called the room. I called Coach Dart. No answer. No Response. So I went down stairs and told the clerk. She called the hotel Manager Mr. Ozark. He asked me have there been other problems with the team. I told him yes they all treat me like they don't like me all the time. He called my coach. No one would answer the phone. Mr. Ozark marched up to the room nearly kicked the door down. And he screamed at my teammates, that I have a right to be in the room just like everyone else and I have a right to be treated equally. He went on to exclaim that if they didn't open the door the school would be penalized. The girls came to the door then and let me in. I called the Old Dirty Hare and told her what had happened. The president of the college said we had to have a meeting when we got back home. And after all of this, I still won a National Award for Impromptu Speaking at the tournament inspite of the coach never practiced me the entire year.

Chapter 14 On My Way Home

On the way home from the tournament, I felt so humiliated. And to make matters worse, Coach Dart asked me to sing the African Hymn that I had been singing in my prose piece all year. I did not hang my harp on the Willow Tree. I sung that Hymn. But I felt tears roll down my eyes. And about a week later after getting back from the tournament, I received a phone call to come to the dean of the communication department office to pick up a letter. Coach Dart had written me a letter removing my scholarship and removing me from the team for talking on the phone during tournament events. He said that he had tried to get in touch with me. I noticed he had never called. But looking a week back into my emails he had sent me a message asking me to come to a meeting. I don't understand why he didn't call when he had my cell phone number and my campus phone number. I called my mom and dad. I called the Dirty Hare. And now I know calling the Dirty Hare was the worst thing I could have done.

She immediately began pressuring me to write an incident report of everything that happened. She said get the witness statements from the motel too. She said this was enough for a lawyer. She wanted me to document every single incident that had happened to me on the debate team from old to new. She told me I had to leave the college and transfer to another school since they had taken my scholarship. I didn't want to go. I was screaming inside don't do it. I was just tired. I was only ten classes away from graduating. And I had helped the Dirty Hare faithfully get her degree. I just wanted to graduate and move on with my life. The Dirty Hare was calling me day and night constantly telling me I had to do it. She drove to my mother's house. She told my mother that I was already bigger than the school. She said that I needed to fight them. My mom told her that her child's education is more important than a political fight. I felt so pressured. And I felt so overwhelmed. The Old Dirty Hare was persistent. So I wrote the incident report. She had me to email it to her. She critiqued it. She said submit it to the dean of Student Affairs but don't tell them I had anything to do with it. She was very clear about not mentioning her name in any of the reports. The Old Dirty Hare had graduated that year too. I listened to her first. I submitted the letter. But then the Old Dirty Hare submitted it to everyone in the community and the NAACP. And they contacted the school to conduct an investigation. The school refused to cooperate. And this is when I begin to be exploited. The Old Dirty Hare begin picking me up from school behind my mother's back and against her wishers, and taking me to NAACP meetings. From there my story was escalated to the highest branch of the NAACP. Then the Old Dirty Hare took me to meet a bunch of old people who were well known Civil Rights Activists in the community. But on all of the paper trail, she insisted that her name not be mentioned anywhere. She said that she was helping me and that she was teaching me how to stand up for myself. And I started to feel so exhausted by this. Like it was getting me nowhere. But the Old Dirty Hare was just getting started. She submitted my letter on my behalf to the American Civil Liberties Union. My God, I don't know what to think of all of this. Then she pressured me into leaving the Christian College and to transfer to the local Public University. She arranged for me to move into a Private Dorm Room over all of the other students who were on the waiting list. And next my case was submitted to the Rainbow PUSH Coalition, and listening to her I submitted it to the EEOC--The Federal Board of Education.

Chapter 15 Missing and Exploited

Somewhere between submitting my claims to all of these organizations and transferring to the new Public University, my friends Tree Top and Flem had gotten expelled from the private Christian College for stealing during Hurricane Katrina. They wrote an article out of retaliation and had it published in the local Media and online. They said the college had a headline saying the college had committed another Racist Scandal. And that's when Tree Top and Flem asked me to join in with their lawsuit they had filed with the American Civil Liberties Union. Some woman named Miranda had brought my name up in the meeting and according to them asked about me to. But I didn't have nothing to do with their case. I was not going to be manipulated into being a Civil Rights Activist. I refused to go down in history as the Black Girl who sued the entire college. And unfortunately for me, everyone around me was pressuring me to be that Black Girl. Everyone minority on the entire campus had heard about my story. People I didn't know, knew my name. It was too much for me. And the Dirty Hare was still keeping tabs on me now only about a potential lawsuit. One day after I had felt a strong urge to give the EEOC investigators the Old Dirty Hare's name as a witness, they called her. The Old Dirty Hare was so shocked. They actually had called her to ask her what did she know about the case. She quickly called me and asked me how did they get her number, and why was they calling her? And I told her, "I gave it to them because I needed your witness statement." I could tell by her countenance she was furious with me. But it didn't seem right that she had went above and beyond to convince me to do all of this even against my mother's wishes, but still not mention her nowhere in the deal. I felt like I was being taken advantage of. I don't know what the Old Dirty Hare said on the phone to the investigator, but my case ended quickly after that. And when she had found out the case was ended, she tried to make me talk to her lawyer friends. And that's when she asked me did I get the witness statement from the motel clerk and manager. But I had had enough of this whole entire ordeal. And I told her no! No! I didn't collect the witness statement and I wasn't going too! And that's when the Old Dirty Hare informed me to my face, that I needed professional help and that she didn't want to be my friend anymore. Just like that I was at a Public University that I did not like or knew anything about and was alone. When the Old Dirty Hare had used me to get her education, and couldn't use me the way she wanted to so she could get rich off of me, she was through with me. People will use you and try to use you up. And when they get you out there so far, they will drop you.

Pray for those who spitefully use you....

Chapter 16 Out of Place

I felt so out of place at the Public University. I was beginning to become depressed. I was still depressed about having to leave the Christian College, losing my scholarship, and how my teammates had treated me and did not receive any reprimandations. I went from 227 pounds to a 155 pounds in three months. I was so sad inside. My heart was grieved. I could not eat although the food in the school cafeteria was the best food I had ever tasted at a school. All I wanted everyday was a smoothie and a turkey wrap. I had unknowingly became a vegetarian. I cried in my private room every night. Tears were my dinner and tears were my breakfast. The people in the dorm beside me would hear me crying. That's when I met Ada. She was a dark skinned thick black girl mixed with Indian.. Her hair was so long that she had to cut it just so weave could be put in her hair. We quickly became friends. Me and Ada and several other girls became friends, including my best friend since High school who lived down the hall. Public School was entirely different from Private. All my peers went to the club every Thursday night. Everyone would spend their extra money to buy the baddest club outfits. And back then, I wanted to be in with the in crowd because it took my mind off of my sorrows. All of us went to the club one night. I didn't have my holy dance back then. I had a body like Buffy the Body and I danced like a stripper. On the club dance floor, Ada decided to try me. In the height of me getting so much attention from the guys, Ada came up to me and started grinding on me. She was bumping her body up next to mine. She was on her knees flicking her tongue out at me. Why? Why Lord did she have to do that? When we got back to the dorm I called Ada to my room. When she walked in I pushed her into the closet door and held her shoulders down. I screamed at her, "Just what in the hell did you mean by bumping your titties up against me in the motha f!@#$%& Club tonight!!!! I don't eat pu$$Y and I don't like pu$$y! If we are going to be friends my advice to you is don't ever try me with that gay $#!+! Understand?" When I let her go she said she was sorry that she just wanted some of the spotlight too. That she didn't mean anything by it. She quickly ran to her dorm room. And then I stopped for a while in my life going to the clubs. But my family began to notice the drastic weight loss. They noticed how for thanksgiving that year I didn't eat a single meal. They noticed how I would go days without eating and sleeping. They noticed how all I talked about was debate this and debate that. They noticed how I begin to wear the same clothes over and over. But they didn't notice how at night I would just hold my pillow over my face and cry.

When I went back to school I decided to sign up for professional counseling. Dr. Webber gave me med samples on the first visit and quickly diagnosed me as depressed. I notice when I came to one of the mixers in the dorms that night, all the other girls thought it would be funny to give me a grocery bag full of condoms. And that's when it started all over again. The girls hated me because I was the new girl on the block with a private room. They had been waiting for years and had not gotten one. On top of that, alot of the guys who were talking to me everyday were involved with them but on the down low. So when no one who would stand up for me was around, I quickly became the target of a bunch of bullies. I hated this school. My grades were surprisingly good, but the environment was terrible. To make matters worse there was Polyester and his brother Brad always at the same places I would be at. Polyester would always be with his new girlfriend who was several months pregnant with his first child. And adjusting to this, the constant bullying, the unresolved mistreatment from the Old Dirty Hare, and going nights without sleeping was too much for me. That's when I went deep in my mind one day. What if I just fell asleep and kept sleeping? Just sleep away. Would I wake up then and be with God? I took eight of the depression pills my Counselor had given me. I called Polyester over to my dorm to hold me one last time before I slept away. He came. And when he saw that I had really took those pills, he ran downstairs and told everyone, including the hall director. Next thing I know the police were at my door questioning me. I fainted. The ambulance rushed me to the local hospital. They checked my blood. But I refused treatment. I ran back to the dorm. I went in my room and I slept for hours. I slept even into the next day. I slept, but I didn't die. I was supposed to die. But death did not find me. I know now that God let me live. Yes I was depressed, but God brought me back for such a time as this. I want you to know that when God has an Assignment on your life, the enemy cannot take your life. And I know that although I was very disturbed at this point in my life, God still had me. He kept me.

He whom I hold in my hand, the devil in hell cannot pluck out! Nothing can separate us from the love of God!

Chapter 17 College Drop Out

My mother had me to withdraw from that school. And just like that I became a college dropout. Just like that my brother's hopes for me of going to law school were all shattered. And when I got home, my school teacher aunt just kept talking about debate teams to me. Why? And every time it would depress me even more. I was a college dropout, kicked off the debate team, and all she would talk about is her engagement in debate activities around me. And this drove me over the edge. I felt like I was a failure. I had dropped out of college in the middle of my senior year. I had no friends. I was at home being constantly reminded of my failure by my aunts and cousins. I did not want to be here. Anywhere but here. And it drove me mad. I begin to walk up the road late night while cars were coming. I begin to give my belongings away to people in my family who I knew did not like me. I did not care to eat, to bathe, or to change clothes. I was saying goodbye. And my mom knew it! She saw that I was saying goodbye. And she had to make a decision. Will I let my child take her life, or will I get her some help even though I know it will stain my child's reputation and credibility? My mother chose for me to live. To live and not die. Even though people would call me crazy afterwards and ostracize me, my mother decided to get me some help. And although I didn't won't to admit it back then, I am mature enough to say now, that I did need help. Coach Dart had shattered my life and my dreams. And I did not know how to pick up the pieces.

I remembered the day I was sent off to get help. They put my hands behind my back. They handcuffed me and carried me off to jail. I was crying Why mom? Why? Don't do this? They place me in a jail cell with no bed or toilet. Just a hole in the floor and a concrete slab. The next day they put an orange suit on me. The one they made people wear when they had murdered someone. They placed shackles on my ankles and handcuffs on my wrists. Why God? Why was this happening to me? Why was I being punished like this? I had committed no crime? And for this part of the mental health process, I blamed my mother; I blamed my family. And I especially hated my mother most of all. I hated her with fury and I did not ever want to live with her or be around her or my family again. I did not know that my mom cried every night I was gone. She came to the county jail to see me every day. She had every preacher in the community praying for me. One man, Pastor Eddie came and found my mother and gave her an anointed prayer cloth that he had prayed virtue into just for me. He told he to place on me and let me take it with me everywhere I go. That she would begin to see God work in my life. I did not know how my mom had so many people praying and fasting for me. I did not know because all I could see was greatly I had been humiliated and been ashamed. I hated my mother and I did not believe in God anymore! I felt like God had forsaken me. And I often asked God why? Why did you let this happen to me God? You know how all I have ever wanted was to be a great lawyer. Why God? Why did you let my dream be snatched away from me? I blamed God for what was happening to me?

There is hope for a fool who knows God is real.

Chapter 18 The Return Home

When I got out the facility, my mom grabbed the bull by the horns. She immediately decided that I was going back to school. She decided that I was going back to the Private College. I hated my mother and I had picked up a rebellious spirit at this point in my life. I told her I was not going back to that school. I know now that my mom loved me. She never stopped praying for me and she never gave up on me, no matter how rebellious I was, how bad I hated the one person who loved me, no matter how bad my attitude was toward her. She had to pay over $500 for me to get back in school. My mom didn't work due to work injuries. She had been trying to get her workman's comp case settled for the last seven years. But somehow, by God's grace, my mom found that money and put me back in school. I absolutely did not want to be there. All of those students who treated me so bad on the debate team were there and Coach Dart. How could I face these people? My mom told me it doesn't matter what happened with them, when I get the same education they have, that shows them I'm strong and that I beat the odds and still won. And that sunk deep in my head. Even though I was still so scared, that sunk in my head.

When I returned home to the Private College, I was only six classes away from my degree. But the classes I needed weren't offered back to back. I had to take them over the time span of a year. But I was still dealing with deep rooted anger against my family. The first thing I tried to do was put as many miles as possible between me and them. I signed up to go on a mission trip in Mexico. Just my luck the news had all kinds of reports of people from our country going over there ending loss and never found. So my mom and my dad refused to allow me to go to Mexico. Then I tried to enlist in the Air Force. Mind you our country was at war on Terrorism at this time. Nope, my mom and my family told the recruiters that I was unstable and not allowed to make decisions like this for myself and for my life at this point and time. And then I begin to get depressed again. Now it probably wouldn't have been so bad if I would have been taking my medication as prescribed, but I refused to take my meds. I would take them every now and then. And that's when I begin to seek comforts in the world. I had to have a man hold me as much as possible. I sought comfort in men, in the clubs, and when my peer introduced me to Malibu rum and peach and pineapple schnapps, I sought comforts in liquor. I became a promiscuous girl. I had my schedule down pack. I would schedule all my classes as night classes on Monday, Tuesday, and Wednesdays. Then I would drink and party the rest of the week every day except Sunday. I partied so much that the other school dropouts did not believe I was still in school. I knew which clubs to go to on what nights that ladies could drink free all night, and get in free. When I arrived at the clubs I would immediately be escorted to the VIP section. One time my mom called me one night and asked me where I was going. I told her I was going to the library. She said she would call me back tomorrow. She just knew I was going to the library to study. But in reality, the club I was headed to was called the Library. I was young and dumb. And I was tearing the clubs up!

One night after coming in at four in the morning from my escapade, I had a dream. I dreamed a beautiful chocolate little girl was getting off the school bus. She was running to me with her arms open wide smiling and screaming Mommy!!! I quickly woke up with this feeling of warmth all over me. Then there was a sudden coldness. Reality had sunk in. Every time I go out on the rendezvous I come home alone. No one to hold me every night. Just another quick thrill. I was tired of coming back to an empty dorm alone. And just like that, I gave up being promiscuous.

I moved into the more upscale dorms across the street with my new roommate T. The school had assigned her to be my roommate. T was on the basketball team. We had nothing in common. She dressed very manly although she had long hair. But things started getting strange when I would come into our room and T would be lying in the bed in just her bra and underwear with her fellow teammate Lindah dressed the same. Infact everyday T and Lindah were in the room together in the bed. One night,

I noticed they were under the covers. I could hear them kissing each other. Even though it was dark, I could see the covers being very busy. I could hear slurping sounds. Oh my God! This was so disgusting to me. Why would they do this in front of me? This kind of behavior went on the entire trimester. One day my mom surprised me and came to my dorm at 8:00 in the morning. I let her in and asked her to be quiet because my roommate and her girlfriend were sleeping. My mom saw them lying in the bed together with no clothes on. And my mom began to protest this out loud. She was so upset. My mom was ranting in loud outburst how this was unfair and not right. She said if people get expelled for girls and boys getting caught having sex in the dorm why should two girls be allowed to do this in front of my daughter! My mother was outraged! I quickly threw my clothes on and escorted my mom out of the room. But my mom would not back down. She had me to take her to the dean of student affairs and report the incidence. My mom was very verbal. And I actually did not disagree. Somewhere deep down, I felt like everything my mom was saying was right. How could they just impose themselves on me like that and not respect me. The Dean was outraged. She immediately called T and Lindah in her office for disciplinary action. And although I just had made new enemies for myself, that stopped lesbian affairs from happening in front of me in my own dorm room. And I can honestly say from my heart, that I strongly believe no one should have to go through that to get an education. It is entirely unethical.

Chapter 19 When the door Closed

Somewhere in my last year of schooling I begin to have problems with my professor. He would not explain the material where I could understand it. I couldn't catch on like the rest of my classmates in the Managerial Finance class. As a result I failed the class. But this was the last class I needed for my Business Administration minor. So I was determined to not give up. I resigned up for the class. This time I signed up for a tutorer. The tutorer wouldn't show up to tutor me. I failed the class again. I signed up for the class again. The school assigned me a tutorer again. She tried to make me understand the business vocabulary. But she did not focus on the math problems. I was failing the class still. I decided to withdraw. I decided to drop the business minor and keep my public relations minor and double major in speech communication and Theatre. I went to the registrar's office to have them audit me again to see what I needed to graduate. They said I could not graduate this year because I had dropped the business minor. They said that I did not have a double major anymore because all of my classes were under speech communication. And just like that everything I had fought for from the beginning of school they had took from me. But I still had a copy of the original catalogue I had enrolled under when I came to the school. I pulled the catalogue and showed them where it said I was in compliance with my degree satisfaction goals. They told me I had to get it approved by the Dean of the department. The department Dean came to the office and personally told them I had satisfied all of my obligations and that he saw no problems in me graduating. But here is the catch, because Coach Dart had blocked me from finishing my final year of debate, the school refused to allow me to graduate with my original double major. Again the Dean of the department intervened. He said if I would take three more classes he would honor the double major fulfillment. The catch was the courses would only be offered over the span of another year. I had been in school for five years. I was tired and I was ready to graduate. So I opted out to just a B.S. degree in Speech Communication and Public Relations Minor.

One day I received a voicemail to come the Dean of Student Affairs office. She said she was concerned about my behavior and wanted to take me off campus herself to get counseling. I told her I needed to talk to my mom first. My mom came over the next day and had a meeting with her. She said they needed to see if I was competent to continue going to school. I was one trimester away from graduating and now this. My mom told her considering how my daughter was treated I say she was very strong to come back here. The Dean told my mother to don't go there. So my mom told her to close your eyes for moment, and imagine a girl who is having an unfair time trying to get her education, imagine a mother who has sacrificed everything for this child to get her education, imagine a school wanting to deny her that right, that's how I feel about my daughter, now I want you to imagine this girl is white. Imagine she is your daughter. Does she deserve a fair chance? That's all we're asking for today-- To give my daughter a fair chance. That's something your school has not given her. Ms. Bren opened her eyes with tears in them. And she told my mother you're right. She said I deserve a fair chance. And she called all my professors and told them that I was competent enough to continue my classes.

When one door closes, God will open another one.

Chapter 20 Graduation

It was in the last trimester of school that I met a man called Black. The first time I saw I was like oh my. He was taller than me, really dark, muscles everywhere, long dreads, and twelve permanent gold teeth in his mouth. He was so fine. Back then that's all I cared about. The first night I met Black we became a couple. He took me places I had never been. I quickly moved off campus with my thought to be best friend Travis. Travis let me share his one bedroom apartment. I paid my part of the rent and helped on the groceries too. When Black would come by to see me which was everyday, Travis gave me privacy. I knew Black had a woman at home, but I felt like that don't have nothing to do with me. And yes he was using her car and her phone and her money to be with me every day. She would call me and curse me out but Black would just take the phone and curse her back out and hang up in her face. But my mom decided Black who didn't work and was five years older than me, was not good enough for me. She had a talk with Travis and from then on Black was not allowed to come to the apartment anymore. So me and Black just went hung out and did our thing in other places. Sometimes in his girlfriend's house too. I was so wrong. And I could have gotten killed.

One day Black took me to meet his mom. The first thing she asked me was I pregnant. I laughed at her and thought she was silly. She said my son don't mind putting babies in women. He has one child due to be born this week. And he has six other children. Black had not told me about any of this. Had I only known. I would have ran like hell!!! The next day Black's girlfriend and five other girls were standing outside me and Travis apartment waiting to jump me. I did not know what to do. Travis grabbed a baseball bat and gave me one. Travis told me that I can't keep hiding in the apartment. He said that I had to stand up for myself. I went outside by myself. Keishia and her cousins circled around me. She asked me why did I bring the bat? I asked her why did you bring all these other girls? I thought it was so wrong for Travis to leave me outside to face them by myself. But I did not know he had made one phone call for my help. Right when things were about to pop off, Travis had an 18 girl squad mixed with straight girls and studs too pulled up for my defense. One of them was packing a gun. They circled around Keshia and her cousins and told her it ain't about to go down like ya'll think. Keishia and her cousins got scared and they backed off. They left. Meanwhile, Travis had called my mother and told her everything that had happened and how he had protected me without me knowing anything about this conversation. The next day my mom showed up to the apartment with my dad and told me I had to go home. They immediately made me move home. Travis called every day to see when I was coming back. My mom said I couldn't come back. That was too much freedom for me and that she did not want me with Black. Suddenly I started wanting to sleep until 3:00 in the evening every day. I would wake up in the morning throwing up every day. You know I could lie to my mother about a lot of things, but this I couldn't hide from her. My mother told me I was pregnant. I didn't believe her. She took me to the doctor and the test revealed I was pregnant. I had just finished all my classes to graduate and not even a week later, I was pregnant.

All of my friends and acquaintances told me to abort my child. My aunt overheard them telling me to abort the child. She pulled into the room and told me that people who abort their children are murderers. We are not murderers in this family. I did not know what to do. I was scared. Pregnant with a child by a man who already had seven other children and who does not believe in working. How would I take care of this child? Back at school, my friends and my peers were telling to abort the child. They said they would help me pay for the abortion. My mom would just cry and tell me no. Please don't abort my grandchild. My dad would even tell me that the child deserves to live. I was scared. I began to remember my roots. I began to remember being raised in the church. I found myself. All of my home training came back to me. I began to read the Bible. I began to talk to God. I made a vow. I asked him to help me take care of this child. I cried out to God more than I had done in the last couple of years of my life. The funny thing about life is you can take a woman who is promiscuous and give her a child. That woman will stand by that child when the father won't. That woman will come out of the streets and raise that child. She will love that child. That child will bring out the best in that woman. And I believe to this day that this is why God gave me this child. Three months later, I marched across the stage four months pregnant. I marched across the stage with the rest of my classmates and received my Bachelor's degree in my hand. Three months later I decided to take the road less traveled by. Inspite of what my friends were telling me, I decided to keep my daughter. And her name would be Zion Moriah. I got my degree in my hand. The president of the college shook my hand when I marched across the stage. This was the first degree of more to come. God had blessed me to get it. The first of my mother's children and grandmother's grandchildren to graduate from college. There I was with my swollen belly waving to my mom and dad. It was then that I decided to take the long road instead of the easy way out. And that has made all the difference.

Tips For College Success

1. Develop good study habits. Read your materials out loud and write important facts down. This will help you memorize quicker.

2. Study for 15 minutes if possible after each class. Studying notes while they're fresh will help retain what you've learned better.

3. Study Abroad if possible. Learning a foreign language can be difficult. After your first two entry level classes a visit to a country that speaks that language will help you become more fluent.

4. Be an active scholar in your classes. Ask questions, give your input on class discussions, and don't be afraid to talk to your professors.

5. Go to bed early. Making sure you have plenty of rest is vital to your education.

6. Take care of your body. Make it a habit while you're young to exercise for atleast 15-30 minutes three days a week. If you take care of your body now, it will take care of you when you're old.

7. If a class is challenging go to Student Support Services and sign up for a tutorer as soon as possible.

8. Start interning and getting experience in your field early. By the end of your Sophomore year you should be starting an internship. Continue to intern all the way through to your Senior year. This will build your resume.

9. If you have complaints, type them and don't be afraid to use the administrative chain of command.

10. Go home as much as possible. However, if home does not provide a healthy environment, try to find a church nearby that will be accepting and supporting of you.

11. Develop a strong prayer life and relationship with God. Prayer changes things. You can start a prayer

journal. Save it. This can be your book. And you can look back and find encouragement.

12. Stay Out Of The Clubs! People in the clubs only go there to look for non-committal sex, over night hookups and to get drunk. Clubs only have one door in and one door out. People fight, shoot, and kill in the clubs. Bullets do not have anyone's names on them.

13. I strongly advise against being promiscuous. When you have sex with someone it opens the door of depression. If you cannot abstain from sex, use protection at all times. Use birth control and always remember, "It Is Better To Marry Than To Burn."

14. Parents—Support your children. Call them every day that you can't be there with them. Visit the campus to see them. Buy them things to reward them and encourage them. Meet all of their professors. If possible, have all of their grades mailed to you. And teach your children how to pray.

15. Fill out your financial aid forms early. At least Six months before you graduate from high school. Talk to your school guidance counselor. Don't shy away from writing intensive courses. A lot of college classes require strong writing skills.

16. Ask about different types of grants like the Pell Grant, SEOG Grant, MTAG Grant. Ask about different types of loans. For example the Perkinson Loan will be paid off for you for every year that you teach at a public school. Ask about subsidized and unsubsidized loans and the Parent Plus Loan.

17. Apply for work study early.

18. Stay on campus. People who live on campus have a higher graduation rate. Stay on campus and familiarize yourself with Student Support Services and your Career Counselor.

Evangelist Sylvia Caver has obtained a great amount of Scholarly Education. She is using this knowledge to help advance the Gospel and the Kingdom of God. Sylvia was called by God in 2012 to reach out to those who are orphaned, widowed, and afflicted. She started Healing Harmony Outreach Ministry. Healing Harmony Outreach Ministry is a licensed nonprofit Christian community service organization that was founded in September of 2012. The purpose of this organization is to love on elderly, nursing home patients, dialysis patients and people who are suffering by sharing the Gospel of Jesus Christ and through our giving. It is the ministry's hope to be a blessing to our community. Today the ministry shares the gospel in many nursing homes in different cities. It also shares the gospel with those who are shut in their homes and need an encouraging word. And it has opened its hearts to praying and interceding for others. Our mission is to be a blessing to our neighbors

Made in the USA
Middletown, DE
22 September 2022

10615117R00038